This Book Belongs to

_____

Published by Lesley Scott & Rachel Rossouw
Copyright © 2020 Lesley Scott & Rachel Rossouw

Amazon ISBN:
979-8-5813-8400-8

Web: www.littlebooksbigfeelings.co.za
Face book: https://www.facebook.com/LittleBooksBigFeelings
Follow us on Instagram: @rachel_rossouw and @les_ct_writes

Sunshine in my Smile

Written by Lesley Scott

Illustrated by Rachel Rossouw

This Little Book is dedicated to
YOU

Remember that it is brave to
feel BIG feelings and to talk
about them.

Hello. I am Pip the Pangolin.
I am mostly nocturnal. That means that I am
usually awake and busy at night!

I have long claws
on my front paws,

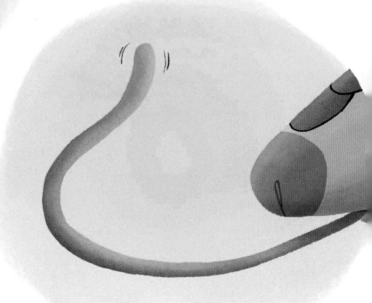

and a very sticky

tongue.

These help me when it's time to find and
catch my yummy termite dinner.

I like to spend most of my time alone. During the day I keep cool sleeping in my underground burrow.

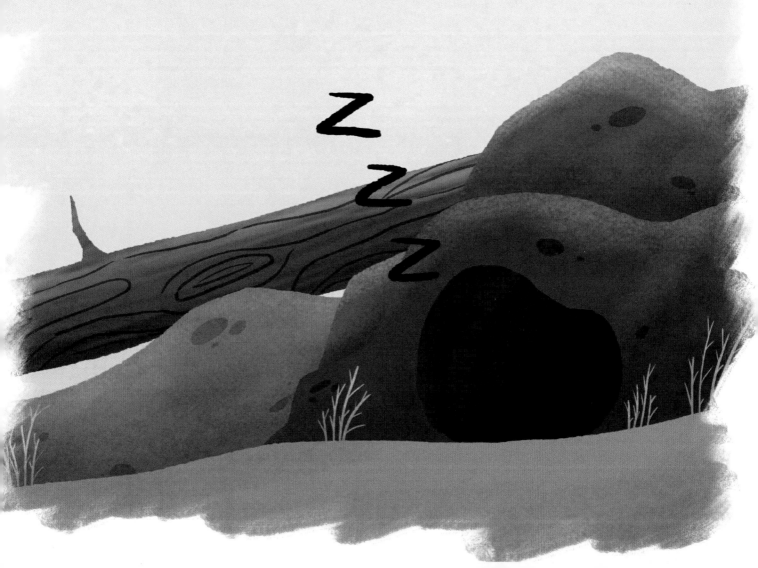

Sometimes I get scared or nervous.
When I feel this way I curl up into a tight ball
so that my tough scales can protect me.

As long as I have a safe place to hide and enough to eat, I am happy.

When I am happy, I am in a good mood.
It is easy to laugh and smile and to do things
that I enjoy.

I may not be happy all the time, but when I am happy I like to think about all the things that make me feel good.

When I am happy, I often feel content. This means that I am calm and peaceful. When I feel like this, I feel good about myself and the world around me.

I like to keep things around me that remind me of happy days.

There are lots of things that I can do that make me happy.

I can spend time with my family and friends.

I can listen to music or sing along.

I can spend some time outside in nature.

I can dance or get some exercise.

I can do something kind for someone else.

I can do silly things that make me laugh.

When I feel sad, angry, or nervous, my happy feelings disappear. It can make me feel as though I will never be happy again.

My mom says that it helps to talk about the things that make us feel bad. When we work on the bad feelings, then we can be happy again.

When I do things for others it makes me happy and makes others happy too.

I can help someone.

I can visit someone who is sad or lonely.

I can invite someone who is on their own to play with me.

I can try to always be kind.

I can give my old toys away to someone who will also like to play with them.

I can look out for small things to cheer me up or I can spend time remembering when I was happy in the past. This can help my happiness find its way back to me.

Reminding myself that I am special and that I have many things to be thankful for helps me to be happy.

Having friends and caring about others makes me feel good inside. We can share our happiness with our friends.

It is good to know that even when I feel bad there are things I can do to help me feel happy again.

If I have friends who are very sad or worried I always tell a grown-up so that they can help them to feel better.

Even being happy can take some work.

When I do things to take care of myself and my feelings, I can be happy more often.

The End

EMOTIONS
HOW AM I FEELING TODAY?

ANGRY

SCARED

ANNOYED

NEUTRAL

HAPPY

UNHAPPY

SAD

Children and happiness – Information for parents

Like all other emotions, happiness is a state of being. Being happy is a feeling of pleasure, satisfaction, or contentment. More intense happy experiences of positive feelings include joy and excitement.

Happiness is a by-product of emotional wellbeing and so it is important to create mental, emotional, and physical habits for children that create the right environment for happiness to thrive.

Why is happiness important?

Research shows that happiness can affect a number of aspects of our life. These include:

- Our health and longevity. Happy people tend to live longer, healthier lives

- Our relationships. Happy people have better quality friendships and romantic relationships.

- Our productivity. We are more productive when we are happy

- Our generosity. It is easier to have a giving spirit when we are happy.

- Our ability to cope with stress. Being happy allows us to find ways of coping in stressful situations.

- Our creativity. Happy people are more creative and are able to see things from multiple perspectives.

- Our sense of self-worth. When we are happy we feel good about ourselves and our place in the world.

How to cultivate happiness in children

- For children it is important to remind them to acknowledge their positive and negative feelings.

- Find the time to laugh and smile. Engage in joyful and silly moments with your child.

- Praise your child and tell them about the good things you see them doing.

- Take time to be outdoors. Nature is one of the best places to find contentment.

- Encourage a child to enjoy their experiences and not just work towards mastering them.

- Practice optimism. Look for the good in every situation.

- Provide opportunities for your child to practice acts of kindness.

- Teach self-discipline and delayed gratification.

- Provide a safe and stable home environment.

- Encourage your child to express their gratitude.and teach them the value of mindfulness (living in the present moment)

- Speak to your GP or paediatrician is you have any concerns bout your child's emotional well-being.

Mental Health Resources

South Africa

(24 Hour crisis & counselling resources)

SADAG (South African Depression & Anxiety Group) 0800 456 789

Suicide Helpline 0800 456 789

Lifeline National Hotline 086 132 2322

Lifeline 021 461 1113

FAMSA 084 666 2095

United Kingdom

Young Minds (Child and Adolescent Mental Health) 0808 802 5544 (Weekdays 9.30-16.00)

Anxiety UK 03444 775 774 (Weekdays 9.30-19.30 Weekends 10.00-14.00)

Samaritans 116 123 (Free call)

Australia

Lifeline 13 11 14

Kids Helpline 1800 55 1800 (For 5-25 year olds)

Suicide Callback 1300 659 467

New Zealand

What's Up 0800 942 8787 (for 5-18 year olds)

Kidsline 0800 54 37 54 (For young people up to 18 years old 24 hours a day)

Lifeline 0800 543 345 For 24 hour access to a counsellor, free call or text 1737

Mental Health Resources (continued)

Canada
  Kids Help Phone 1 (800) 668 6868
Canada Suicide Prevention 1 (833) 4566

USA
NAMI 1-800-950-6264
Lifeline 1-800-273-8255
Text teen-to-teen to 839863 for teen-to-teen crisis support
Parental Stress line (800)632-8188

 (These contact details are accurate at date of publishing)

Made in the USA
Las Vegas, NV
08 October 2024

96510100R00021